FORTY POEMS FOR CITY LIVING

Pilsen-18th Street

FORTY POEMS FOR CITY LIVING

Pilsen-18th Street

Joel Méndez

MARCH
MARCH ABRAZO PRESS

LACASA CHICAGO
Latin American Latin@ Cultural Activities and Studies Arena

Joel Méndez 1950

Cover art: "Reach for Peace." 2011. Yollocalli Arts Reach, youth initiative of the National Museum of Mexican Art. Chucho Rodríguez, lead teaching artist. Location: Taquería Los Comales 1544 W 18th Street Chicago, IL 60608.

ISBN: 978-1-877636-14-1
Library of Congress Control Number: 2023916496
Listed in the Catalogue of the Library of Congress: 1. Literature 2. Poetry. 3. U.S. and Chicago Mexican and Chicano Literature. 4 Ethnic Literature. 5. Urban Literature. 6. Neighborhood Literature. 7. Chicago Mexicans. 8. Latinos

LACASA Chicago Books
2120 W. Concord Place,
Chicago, IL 60647
www.lacasachicagobooks.org
mzimmerman1939@gmail.com
And/Or: marchabrazopress@yahoo.com

For all past, present, and future
residents of Pilsen, Chicago

A very special thank you to
Marc Zimmerman and Carlos Cumpian
for believing in me and encouraging me
to get my poetry published. Thank you
for your expert advice and professionalism.

Contents

Foreword

FORTY POEMS FOR CITY LIVING evokes a time, place, and life that refuses to be gentrified. Like a tree whose intricate roots run deep, powerful neighborhood images disrupt ongoing attempts to displace a vibrant past and resistant present with the objective of developers, the transformation of an immigrant community into an ethnic Disneyland. The poems in this collection provide a bridge to understanding what went before, an important task, since without a past there is no meaning. Without an authentic context, history can easily be reduced into a mythological space to support any number of manipulative narratives that can anchor ideological illusions like the "American Dream."

Joel Mendez provides us with **sense-making touchstones**: rat-filled alleys, the ever-present danger of the street; life beneath the shadows of skyscrapers, and the backroom machinations of City Hall and La Salle Street. There are the homeless, the lost; those who want and whose needs are unlikely to be met. Yet, there are also true friends; the fond memories of those no longer present; family and the assuring sound of a mother's voice; the spaces of freedom, the laughter in the park, Saturday nights, and the promise of spring. All these images comprise the elements of youth and the architecture of a Mexicano-Chicano's life growing up in a working-class community.

FORTY POEMS FOR CITY LIVING links us to what is authentic and valuable. They are the memories that refuse to be tortured into someone else's projection of who we are, who we should be, and what we have lived. It is an attempt to stake a claim on a truth that is embedded in our experience and stays in our memory. It is necessary to make this process intentional to resist the alluring notions and intoxicating master narratives that threaten to gentrify not only our pasts but our souls. Joel Mendez has given us guideposts to help us along the way to our own process of liberation.

Leonard Ramírez, PhD.

Invocation

Chicago is a microcosm of immigrants from around the world and from all walks of life. It is a city where multi-ethnic working class enclaves thrive in distinct neighborhoods. Contrary to common belief, Chicago is not a melting pot. Instead, the city is a tapestry made of many different cultures, languages and nationalities stitched together to give the city its unique character and cosmopolitan flair.

The poems in this book are based on memories and first hand experiences while growing up in Pilsen and Chicago's Near and Lower West Side. It's an area where Latino/Hispanic (primarily Mexican and Puerto Rican), African-American, Italian, Greek, Czech, Polish and many other ethnic Eastern European residents still live shoulder-to-shoulder in search of their own dreams while zealously holding on to their ancestral roots.

Chicago has never been static, and it continues to go through changes. By the time I came of age in 1968, "white flight" had begun. The neighborhood that I knew and grew accustomed to was also changing fast welcoming new residents and displacing many of the old ones who were moving on (often reluctantly) to 'better' parts of Chicago and nearby suburbs.

As you read these vignettes of inner city life, I hope you will recall some of your own personal experiences while growing up and coming of age in your own city or town neighborhood –just as I have done.

Joel Méndez

I. WE WERE THERE

DREAM RERUN

Black and white images
of crooked cops
chasing me down
the narrow trash-filled alley
shouting my name
blaming me for mischief
I did not commit.

I don't look back

            I zig-zag
I search
      I keep running

I keep searching…

for a quick getaway in the spaces
between the old brick buildings
ignoring the warning calls to stop.

But a gut-wrenching feeling
urges me to keep running.

Friends and neighbors stare;
they think I've lost my mind.

I don't look back
            I keep running
and then,
        I wake up

And realize (in relief)
it was just the same
recurring dream messing
with my slumbering mind… again.

CAR RADIO

A child-traveler dreams
in a lonesome two-lane
road marked in red ink
linking Texas to Chicago.

Two long days immersed in
bouncy songs flowing in and out
of the two-tone (cream and green)
'54 Ford's crackling car radio

crooning rock n' rolling
teen idols' love songs,
country n' western ballads,
and jazzy St. Louis blues that

finally meld with sweet soul
Motown chart busters –hit after hit
marking the end of yet another
road trip to the hip urban north.

All through the long journey
the child-traveler's place was always
in the back seat with blanket-covered
sisters and brothers always sleeping…

DECONSTRUCTING JESÚS

Jesus? Did you write Jesus?
Your name cannot be Jesus.
What kinds of parents name a child Jesus?

We must call you something else…

My friends call me Chuy.
You can call me Chuy.
That's my nickname –Chuy.

Never mind *that*…
You live in America.
We'll call you Jesse because
you can never be Jee-zus.

JEEZUS? That's not my name, ma'am!

Well, my real name is Jesús.
You can just call me Jesús.
My name in Spanish is Jesús.

Hay-zoos?… No, that won't do.

You live in 'Merica, boy!
Your name from now on is Jesse.
You are not Jesus. That's for sure.

Get that through your fourth-grade…
Mexican head.

WHEN PILSEN WAS 18

YOU WERE THERE

playing hockey in its streets
countless winter days
thinking like a Blackhawk
and swinging your crude
stick hard–like a pro
in the steely gray
ice-covered asphalt.

YOU WERE THERE

when spring
arrived dressed in green
with a florid face
and you happily
prepared for
a fresh game
of softball
at Dvorak Park
and held your breath
expecting your friends
(and a certain girl you fell for) to show up.

YOU WERE THERE

loving the days getting longer
as the summer's heat
rolled in like a giant
beach ball and you made
your way to the Throop
Street ball court
bouncing to the beat
of "Jumpin' Jack Flash" blaring
out of your portable
blue radio pinned
on the Park District's
tall green wire fence.

YOU WERE THERE

cooling off your teenage temper
at the corner fire
hydrant decorated
in car tires that
shimmered when wet.
There, you raised the thin
translucent water
curtain that showered
down on you and all
the joyful soggy
children of the block;
the air was filled
with laughter and song
while the stream of
cold water refreshed
as it splashed on their smiling faces.

YOU WERE THERE

acting as the official
water pump dispenser
clasping the torrent
of white water by
locking the fingers
of your wide-open
hands as your biceps
bulged out of the wet
sleeve-less frayed tee shirt
clinging like clear tape
on your swollen chest.

YOU WERE THERE

waiting
to greet September's
sudden arrival
flanked by howling winds
rolling street rubble
like tumbleweed down
Eighteenth Street announcing
the start of the World
Series on your rabbit-eared TV
and you wished the Sox would
slash the Detroit Tigers for you.

YOU WERE THERE

in your third-floor flat living
room slumped in the red
sofa-bed covered

in clear plastic.
Your eyes were glued
to the black and white
TV screen and when
you felt the chill of
the shifting autumn
winds you then got
the itch for a game of
football with the boys and
you played better than the Bears.

YOU WERE THERE

on that particular
late October night when
you took a lungful
of urban blue air and looked
out of your bedroom
window and gazed at
the autumn moon – big and
round as an orange
hanging in the star
glittering sky and you
silently wished that
your life on 18th Street,
–the beating heart of Pilsen–
would last forever... *pa 'siempre.*

THERE WE WERE

Days of Rage
crisscrossing the nation.
Daily media frenzy over the '68
Chicago Democratic Convention.

The world was not watching
18th and Throop Streets
Corner where time stood still.

Hopeful coming-of-age *camaradas.*
Hands in their bottomless pockets.
Future uncertain and hanging loose
just waiting… just hoping…
just hanging in the corner…

Chapters in the Annals
of Undocumented History
were being written
and nobody noticed...

Chicago's Finest were
making their rounds.
Their motto: Serve and Protect
strictly professional (so they say)

Decisions were made –on the spot—
Purpose: create some local excitement
justify *Pigotry's* authority
and no one said a word…

Suspicion –always the excuse.
Humiliation the expected reaction.
All for a good laugh, of course
at the expense of unsuspecting fresh meat
                    and the *show* would go on…

Spreading of legs and bashing of hands.
Billy clubs up the innocent's buttocks.
Bodies against graffiti-filled walls.

Unwilling eyes passing through
confirming the search for fictional
guns and drugs and alcohol
                    and no one took note…

Anger flared up
wise guys in the squad
taken for a ride

                    and no one took note…
And…
          There We Were in '68…

RECUERDOS

(Mother's Day in the neighborhood)

Who…
calmed your throat and cured your cough
dried your tears and wiped your nose?

Who…
caressed your face and cleaned your hands
subdued your fears and cried for your losses?

Who…
felt your pain and remembered your birthday;
overlooked your faults and forgot your mistakes?

Who
suffered your losses and celebrated your gains;
fought for your rights and believe in your causes?

Who
mended your broken heart and gave you hope,
prayed for your safety, and blessed all your triumphs?

Who
gave you birth and heartfelt love with unexpected return
and…
still waits all night long for you to come home?

At this very moment somewhere in the neighborhood
somebody's mother is still doing it all for her children
living in the third-floor rear apartment.

TIME MACHINE

My last
wish before
I leave
this present
frame of mind
is to hop
on a time
machine
that would
swiftly
lunge me
non-stop
into my past
teleporting
me back
to nineteen
sixty-eight
to that
familiar place
where I
find myself
walking
down a
crowded
street
feeling
carefree
wearing
my favorite
Italian knit
sharkskin

wrinkle-free
straight leg
pants and
shiny black
leather shoes
while holding
my transistor
radio playing
all my long
forgotten
soulful
love songs.

I REMEMBER

Sitting in the rear seat
of the metallic blue
two-door ’64 Chevy
Impala. Windows closed.
It was the night before
Christmas as we waited
for Casanova to return
with some festive girls.

Ace, whom we had
just met was sitting
next to me smelling
like a bottle of Old
Spice took a slug
of Canadian Club
and said he was
an Almighty King.

That’s when Louie
turned his head
and began to preach
about God being
the one and only Almighty.

Louie pointed his finger
at Ace and spoke
in that low tone of his
and told him that
there is nobody
mightier than God

Ace said, "Well you
are looking at
an Almighty King!"

Right then and there
is when my fist landed
square in Ace's face
just to see…
        if he was for real.

CRAZY JOE

One fine day
Crazy Joe
climbed up
to the rooftop
of his third floor
flat apartment

Joe said he wanted
to prove to everybody
the Nine Lives Theory
wrong once and for all,
He was right.

I guess he is not
so crazy after all,
just cracked
like the poor cat
lying flat like
a fresh corn tortilla
in the red-stained sidewalk.

MEN ON THE MOON

Back in ‘69
we were there
in our street corner
roosting like crows
all dressed in black.

We hung tight and low
near the candy store
next to the red fire
hydrant just in case
the night got excited
and we needed to cool down
our urban hormones stashed
in the breast pockets
of our three-quarter length
black leather coats.

We were there, lost in our youth.
We looked at the stars and tried
to imagine ourselves as the spacemen
who took giant steps to stake
our American flag in the moon.

But all we could see was old
Uncle Sam looking for bait
to send to Hamburger Hill
where bombing and shelling
raged in full force without pity.

The night was still young and
when you happened to pass by
our street corner, you made sure
to make it all the way
to the tattered stop sign
carrying a brown-wrapped
bottle of juice and some squares.

We had the light and the latest soul hits
playing in our portable radio and,

yes, we felt we had…
                    all the time in the world.

BACK PORCH DREAMERS

A blue moon dances with the clouds
while distant stars play their role
as beacons in the vast night
lighting dormant
dreams floating
in the crossbeams
of porch landings
yearning for the dawn
sun to rise.

Slippery back porch stairs to nowhere.
Buzzing bugs compete for a slice
of recycled air
like a piece of leftover pie.
Thirsty alley weeds
and rustling trash thrive
in the concrete cracks
of the empty parking lot
nestled between decaying walls of
the abandoned factory
proclaimed the official
resting place of random bullet holes.

Rancid wine, pungent
weed, and soulful radio songs
slice the stale summer air while
a confused adolescent sleeps
under the moldy basement stairs.

A self-imposed young lookout
remains motionless in position
like a vigilant stone not worried
about tomorrow's divine scheme.

There will always be dreamers
coming to the back porch.

BARRIO DOGZ

Droopy-eyed street mutt,
ignore the police sirens;
forget the wailing ambulance.
Come on, shed your tears
and shake my open hand.

Feel my grip, get comfortable;
mine is not the kind of hand that bites.
I understand you were gambling
for crumbs not too long ago and now
you're lying face-up at the bottom

of the pit you fell into and you're looking
for help from strangers holding
musty greenbacks and luring you out
of your hole with temptations that are
the envy of many and the prize of few.

I've seen you lots of times
just lying there in the dark, wounded
feeling like nothing beneath
the brightly studded sky,
as you watch the phases
of the moon pass you by.

I've seen your sad eyes
sail across the twilight and
witness the sun rise
above the parabolic dishes
protruding out of tar-smeared rooftops

connected to home screens that numb
the minds of children and tempting
them with false dreams
of riches and happiness
they gladly embrace.

I, too, once had such sweet fantasies
that led to twisted ways and bad days.

So get moving and let's shake
hands again. Let me see your mangy
face and wounded eyes.
Let me assess the damage written
in the scars you carry on your sides.

Let's see how your tell-tale lines compare
to mine. Let's figure out how we can both
come to terms as to what
our next move will be tonight.

Life in the neighborhood ain't always pretty…

GHETTO SHOES

At first, they were known
everywhere as *sneakers.*
Inexpensive and meant to be
for the working class but
the chic and trendy noticed
so, they became our *tennis shoes.*

Then, the marketing gurus
joined the name-game and
tag-labeled them *gym shoes*
for schoolers and s*ports shoes*
for the jaunty and trendy jet set

And then, the brokers and stockholders
gladly saw their profits soar…

Nowadays, Wall Street greed and
Fifth Avenue stiffs are in control.
Self-absorbed vultures sitting
in their corporate boards
flock together concocting
ritzy promises and Hollywood dreams

of fame and luxury to fit our feet
and feed our flaunting attitudes
while third world children in bare feet
mass-produce our ghetto shoes
packaged neatly in fancy sporty boxes
and we hear them now called …

Athletic shoes!

INDIANA LUPE

One night while jousting at the club
I met a girl named Guadalupe.
She was made of cinnamon and spice
exquisite full lips and almond eyes.

We struck on deep conversation
and shared our views on life.
She told me she felt stupid among
predatory drunken souls in search of love.

As she spoke, velvet petals filled the air and
feathered serpents emanated from her eyes
but then, what struck me most was her disgust
with—Of all things-- tortillas! Yes, TORTILLAS!

So I asked her… "Why?",

"Well, for the most," she said,
"they remind me of who I am."

Hey, that's self-hatred, girl!

I tried to be persuasive and explain
But… I soon realized
she didn't seem to give a damn

about anything I had to say;
her mind was done made up

So, I waved good-bye and
wished her no less
in her quest (I guess) for …
“enriched” white bread.

IN MEMORIAM: MAXWELL STREET

Dented garbage cans stand tall
like strategically positioned pawns
on litter-checkered empty lots
belching glowing cinders
and undecipherable smoke signals
into a bustling Maxwell Street…

The scent of crackling firewood.
A miscellany of burning skeletal
remains that once were fancy tables,
rocking chairs, and sofa beds.

The aroma of grilled onions,
fat-fried pork chops, and
mustard-splattered Polish
sausages and hot dogs,
Greasy fries and pickled relish.
Pungent but pleasing
smells that work their way
into unsuspecting runny cold noses
leading ever-vigilant onlookers
in search of bargains in storefronts,
sidewalk tents and makeshift stands
filled with neatly folded second-hand
blue collar shirts and khaki pants,
pimp oils, bedroom trinkets and
worn-out barroom artifacts.

The hawking eyes of Black, Brown and
White sweaty faces avidly scanning
for lost treasures among piles of

plumber's tools and carpenter's glues,
faded lamps and dining table sets,
bent forks and ornate spoons,
workman's shoes and oily screws,
rusty nails and fishing nets, sinkers,
hooks and blunted knives.

The winos, bums, pimps and ladies
of the night seem to beg onlookers
to stop and listen to lifelong stories
engraved in the cuts and bruises
they all commonly displayed.

The busty Gypsy women in low-cut blouses
luring men –of all ages— into dark hallways
leading to nebulous up-the-stairs spaces
saturated with musty incense where
giggling Gypsy girls eagerly await
to try out their fortune-telling
talents and other games of prey.

The chunky Indian lady dressed
in ostrich feathers and amulets brandishing
her ten-foot boa constrictor
slithering around her neck
Like a necklace juxtaposing
her flowery grease-stained dress.

The tall leathery Blackman
with the rooster on his head
Walking proudly down the street
relishing the stares he gets from
Black, Mexican, and Puerto Rican boys

dressed in worn out clothes
with their fingers clenched to mothers'
hands and their little feet kicking up dirt
with their hole-in-the-sole shoes
as they stride by the crowded way.

The cacophony of sounds interlacing
MLK's, *I Have a Dream* and JFK's
Ask Not Inaugural Address with
dusty melodies of sweet soul oldies
and Norteño lyrics doused with
bajo sexto and acordeón.

The strumming steel guitar and hollow
sounds of a broken drum and snare
of scraggly bluesmen in their ragged suits
scuffed Stacy Adams and
worn-down patent leather shoes.

The raspy voice of a wine-scented
Black woman flaunting a dusty wig;
her neck enveloped in a hot pink scarf
hanging low, wa-ay low, down to her knobby knees
as if covering from sight a stained-stiff miniskirt
and unraveling fishnet stockings wrapped
around her wiry lower limbs. She sings
the blues like no one else could. Pouring
out her heart and setting the mood
out in the street for those that care to listen
to the pains and joys of the good life
she once lived and now gone too soon…

The final stop –always a treat--

at *Lindo México. An o*asis
of familiar kitchen sights
and smells. Fresh tortillas,
luscious salsas, steaming barbacoa,
succulent carnitas, kickass jalapeños,
rice and beans, and crunchy chicharrones.
A place where a memory-making meal
never fails to appeal to the need
for a dish of succulent tacos
and endless cups of café con leche.

Contrary to hearsay commonly believed
(whenever I describe this scene)
this vignette is not a dream…
It's a living memory
of a bustling Maxwell Street –a
long-lasting part of the city in me.

So, Mayor Daley and accomplices--
including UIC-- I say to you:
While you have done away
with what once was the magnet
of Chi-Town's Near Westside,
Maxwell Street remains forever in my heart
I shall not forget… I shall not forget

Jew Town!
        La Garra!
                14th and Halsted!

QUE VIVA MAXWELL STREET!

II. HERE WE ARE

A DAY IN THE CITY

An elderly woman and her man hold each other's arthritic
hands.
Their shaky legs move slowly feeling for bumps on the
uneven sidewalk.
A trail of aromatic *Bengay* and *Alcoholado Relámpago**
permeates the air
they leave behind. They continue to believe the contaminated
city
water is responsible for their body aches and pains.
Their mission today: the corner drugstore.

Down the street, in a trash-covered empty lot nestled
between two dilapidated three-story brick buildings, two
teen crows have skipped school. Filled with excessive
energy, they hip hop and wobble along with swollen chests.
To kill time, they playfully spew radioactive green
testosterone
at each other's second-hand imitation leather coats.

Across the street an oversized digital clock hangs and sways
above the corner's food & liquor store flashing the current
time telling all passers-by that the scheduled ICE raid
has been postponed to return another day.

The good news for tonight is there will be no crying babies.
Everyone on the block will finally get some overdue sleep.
Tomorrow will be just another day at the sweat shop. Bus
fare is set aside and the store-bought sandwiches are packed.

Meanwhile, down at city hall an honorable jolly
walrus dressed in a sparkling pink Barbie tuxedo
sips his coffee and puffs on his smuggled Cuban cigar.
Above his head a red spangled banner
screams in blue letters…
"All Immigrants are Welcome!"

* *Mentholated/medicated rubbing alcohol*

MORNING DRAG

The day opens its eyes
across the quiet horizon.
The city yawns and wiggles
her dew-covered slippery jaws.

The streets are still, hollow, and silent;
the lamp posts sigh and shut their eyes
to fuse with the rapidly vanishing stars

Serene and slippery as a panther,
darkness waits on the ledge
of the single pane window
awaiting its final surrender to the daylight.

The blue-collar class lying
face down in bed remains
covered in warm sheets holding on
to twilight dreams in their final act
postponing the end of their dreams and wishing
for the delay of the awaiting working day.

Meanwhile, down in the kitchen,
the coffee pot noisily emanates
its irresistible aroma.

PILSENESQUE

People move to their own vibrant beat
up and down a bustling 18th Street.
Flanked by weather-worn buildings
standing tall like ancient walls built of
baked bricks made a century ago.

The street gleams in its debonair style.
Tree-lined sidewalks and antique lampposts
Invite passers-by to stop and shop for a cup
of café con leche y un pan dulce keeping
the neighborhood's old ways alive.

A noisy line of cars parades the busy strip
decked out in ribbons and blaring their horns.
Dressed-up riders wave their hands held up high,
sidewalk spectators cheer them back while
the happy newlyweds raise their arms up to the sky.

As the riding entourage disappears
the festive mood lingers in the empty street
and countless murals reappear screaming
in technicolored designs proclaiming
the local culture and artistic pride.

Young ladies dressed to impress
crisscross the bustling street while
bike riders turn and catch a glimpse.
The long-awaited city bus slowly nears
and the old riders react with shopping bags held tight.

While the echo of the fading nuptial parade
loiters longingly in the buzzing urban air,
trading final notes with the booming music
blasting through the plugged ears of stragglers
waiting at the crowded bus stop bench.

NEW MILLENNIUM CLUB

Bouncing shadows
dancing wild
at the Sports and
Salsa nightclub…

The rhinestone
studded DJ shuffles
his own hot mix
as he syncs
the booming beats
to the over and over
music-video scenes

As abject poverty
from a another
world reality
is flashing on
the giant
HD screens.

An oblivious
tipsy flock
of countless
silhouettes
moving arms
shuffling legs
bumping hips
and high-heeled feet
minds drunk
with the rhythms
and the flashing
strobe-light beams
pointing at
the action in
the dancing rings.

And not one
single dancing
soul cares to
stop and look at
the vivid
image of
the child by
the roadside
blown to bloody bits
by a roadside IED*

The club music
keeps bouncing
off the walls and
the dancing goes on
until dawn while our
military presence
in the distant desert
continues to explode.

So, I walked away
shaking my head
wondering what
in hell was that
stone-studded DJ thinking.

**Improvised Explosive Device*

ALTERED STATE

Again…
I use
I lose
I bleed
I beg
I plead
I break
No cure
Too late
We need
We crave
For joy
For lust
We fly
We live
You take
You try
You find
You lose
You use
Again…

Life in the neighborhood isn't always pretty…

MANIFESTO FOR DÍA DE LOS MUERTOS

I.
In spite of all the hoopla
being fed by our usual
trendy American ways
unwittingly making one
more commercialized day,
we must resist and celebrate
Like we've done in the past.
It's part of our history and culture
not a Halloween contest…
(Disney tried to appropriate the Day)

II.
Let the Day be as it should.
No outlandish Catrinas
or fancy-dressed Fridas
No China-made cheap
trinkets from Walgreens or
Walmart usurping the Day.

III.
Be sure the candles are lit
lighting up the altar
and all the fine features
of fading old photos still
hold the power to bring back
lost smiles and dormant vignettes
of memorable seasons and dated events.

IV.
Be sure the Marigolds call the spirits
and sweet lemongrass is ready
for tea and papel picado highlights
the table and the altar presents
La Virgen Morena and Cristo
Jesús –both flanked right and left
by a legion of the family santos
greeting our loved souls coming
safely back to our earthly confines.

V.
Be sure the copal is smoldering to
enhance the air for all visiting souls
and grain salts are sprinkled so
our lives safely continue on Earth.

VI.

Be sure freshly-baked pan de muerto
and home-made sugary skulls and
agua fresca in glass pitchers are all
ready to appease all traveling souls.
Don't forget the tray of clay jarros
filled to the brim with atole.
The bowl of spicy-sweet mole.
A stack of blue corn tortillas.
Arroz blanco and pozole.
Green and red chiles.
Cheese quesadillas.
The bowl of dry cereal.
Ripe freckled bananas.
Strawberries and sweet cream.
Oranges, pineapple, dry figs.
And straight from old México,
peeled sweet mangoes splattered
with chile… inviting tongue-licks.

VII.

Be sure a bottle of mezcal Mixteco
with its meaty worm is ready
to be served in tío Beto's
still sparkling original set
of hand-painted shot glasses.

VIII.
Be sure there on the table is abuela's
black wooden charola
brought home from Zamora
holding quarter-sliced limes
to enhance the glow in both
the dead and the living enjoying
the toasts of tequila and wine
flowing down their thirsty dry throats

IX.
Be sure all day long and into the night
we rapture and share fond memories
and chit-chat and laugh
and cry and pray and listen
to primo Panchito's guitar
and gaily sing and dance
to our favorite songs
as we honor the long-
awaited return of all
our beloved ancestors
coming to us once again
from their ethereal abode.

X.

And at the end of the day be sure
that together we pray in sing-song
to all of Creation and thank once
again, for all our blessings brought forth
by the Day of the Dead that is
a part of our history and culture and
not a Halloween contest.

URBAN WINTERLAND

Snow is back in the Windy City
so fresh so shiny and so clean
covering the grime and hiding
all hints of white-collar crime.

Snowflakes in mid-air frolic and lay
a fluffy ivory sheet in the streets
and sidewalks and frosting the tall
smart city lamps blurring the urban decay.

Six-corner flakes of infinite shapes land
on slanted rooftops, morph into teardrops
trickle down the wet eaves turn into spikes
cascade above front doors and wait to
stabs folks fixed on their cell phones.

In the lone city park the glittering fluff
settles to cover and snuggle the grass
hiding tell-tale stains of empty beer
cans and shattered bottles of wine.

Clumps of alabaster hang on the branches
of evergreens and the naked arms of black oaks
brighten the Christmas-lit crab apple trees
heralding a joyful and peaceful holiday glee.

Whenever fresh snow dresses the city
it always succeeds in bringing brief joy to tired
red eyes before urban delight turns
into smut all over again…

BARRIO SIDDHARTHA

There's a *veterano* with a scraggly
speckled beard wearing
a hand-me-down all black
White Sox baseball cap
and torn recycled pants…

He holds steadfast a waxed paper cup
of coffee in his exposed right hand
and a lit cigarette in his left.

He told me he finally
got the Divine Call to
unplug forever decades
of bondage for far too long
dictating his day-to-day
meaningless urban ways.

He left behind the billionaire's
incorporated production line
stained with worn workers'
blood and salt-sweaty grime.

He left behind the constant
deafening clockwork tick-tock
and that dreaded daily need
for a gasp of clean fresh air.

He will no longer worry
about having to respond
with a YES when in his heart
he always meant to say NO.

He knows it's up to him alone
to reject the things that he can't
accept or postpone the things
that he no longer can condone.

He walks away with his
salvaged dignity. It is
the only thing he has left
to feed his purpose for living.

The crowded streets burst
with clock-like human drones
tempting him to return to the
empty space he left behind
in his old workplace.

But today he still stands steadfast
and ready to become
a bona fide street-trekking
monk in search of Nirvana
for his convalescing city soul.

SUMMER NIGHT

Sultry dark scents lure the rodents out
as sweat-beaded faces shake their bony
arms and roam the city with matching red
eyeballs scanning the summer night.

Tired ears listen to the gnawing
at the scraps homeless children hide for
another day in an abandoned car.

Robocops and undercover private door-
shakers wearing sacred badges prey on
clueless souls sleeping in darkened storefronts.

The graveyard shift tic-tocs away
the clammy night and the insomniacs pretend
to dream under the buzzing neon lights.

The *Lord of Mictlán* and his lovely
wife take aim at the street corner's rowdy
crowd with their double-barreled spray cans
of *Made in China* black rodenticide
seeking justice in the streets tonight.

Meanwhile, dizzy roaches wave their white flags.

FELIZ NAVIDAD

Near the entrance to the corner
drugstore a stalwart gray-haired
venerable woman relentlessly twitches
her bruised left eye as she swings
her good arm and repeatedly rings
a bright silver bell from side to side.

A wiry and hunched aging man
wearing a skull cap and weathered
brown face wrapped in a navy-blue scarf
drops a coin in the hungry red pot.

Not far behind is a blue-haired finicky-faced
feline swishing her bushy striped
tail in mid-air proudly displaying
her fluffy fur coat and shiny red bag
splotched with green dollar signs.

She shrugs her padded shoulders and
fastidiously meows as she arrogantly skirts
the rhythmic melodious arm swaying
and ringing its cheerful holiday charm…

And we hear the bell ringing to the tune of
Feliz Navidad!

MIGRANTE (Diáspora)

Eres tu
las ramas
que se
entrecruzan
y divergen
en el verde
árbol de la vida

Creces
sin descanso
rumbo al Eden
donde no
existen
fronteras
artificiales

Engendras
semilla y
forjas tu
fruto fértil
plantándolo
en el oscilante
vientre de
la vida

Y sigues
de frente
hacia las
cuatro esquinas
de la Madre
Tierra bañada de sol

Pero tus
antiguas raíces
siguen siendo
una sola vena…
  pura
    honda
      fuerte
        profunda.

Es por todo
esto que
debes
asegurar
que tus hijos
y los hijos
de tus hijos
conozcan bien…

  los hombros en que se sostienen.

MIGRANT (Diaspora)

You are
the branches
crisscrossing
and diverging
in the green
tree of life.

You grow
relentlessly
skyward to Eden
where there
are no artificial
borders.

You bear
seed and
forge your
fertile fruit
planting it in
the oscillating
womb of Life

And you
take the lead
and move
onward to
the four
corners of
our sun-
drenched
Mother Earth.

But your
ancient
roots remain
as one vein…
pure
  deep
      strong
         profound.

It is because
of all this that
you must
make sure
your children
and your
children's children
know well…
the shoulders they stand on.

BACK TALKIN'

You done did it again!
Didn't I tell you? Didn't I?

But, no-o-o, you had to go out there
And show your machismo by
Shoveling snow like there was
No end to your pubescent charade.

Yes, but...

NO. No no-no. No-o. Don't even go there.
There are no ands or buts about it
you just don't care for your back... and for it
you're gonna pay –dearly.

YOU-ARE-GOING-TO-PAY-FOR-IT-BABY!

You're gonna feel the hurt
down to your sorry ass tail bone.
Yes, you're gonna pay your debt
I'm making sure of that –before I'm gone.

Ok, ok, ok. Get out of my face, will you?

What’s the matter with you?
You ain’t no spring chicken any more, son.
Did you forget that? Whaddaya think?
I’m made of steel and stone?
I am your fragile and tired back bone.

Oh baby, I’m tellin’ you old man
I’m gonna talk to you tonight
‘till you’re blue in the face
You just watch. You better hold tight!
I’m kiddin’ you not.

Yeah sure, whatever.

BEAR'S CALL

Rrr-ring!…
Rrr-ing!

Hey, Bear!
Is that you?
Yeah. How's it going?
Everything's cool.
Glad to know.
How's it with you?
OK, I guess…

Gigging?
Yeah. Well …no.
Looking around?
No, just laying low.
Taking a break?
Got no choice.
Don't wait too long.
Ain't desperate, 'bro.
Not yet.
Till the money's gone.
That won't take long…

Well … I better go.
Yeah, me too.
See you later.
Yeah, thanks for the call.
Adios.
G'bye.

Click!

REQUIEM FOR SLIM*

Gone with the winds of time
are those paperboy days
when you teased me
about the girls that stood
by the stoop next to your cantón
waiting for me to come along…

Years later you'd bring it
up and teasingly remind me
how much a neophyte
I was back then.
Yeah, it was all in the fun
of growing up and coming of age
in the barrio were we
became more than friends.

"Carnales to the bone!"
you would say as we
sipped from our
brown-bagged bottles
and sang Motown
to the radio in your car.
Jammin 'to Billy Steward's
Sitting in the Park and
Fat Boy (hey, that was you!)
Forever joking, dreaming, polkeando,
Living the good life (so we thought)
Yeah! We were fearless and saw
ourselves as big time studs.

We entered adulthood.
Reality set in and you were gone

to fight in a war
that wasn't yours nor mine.
From the get-go you held
your head high and served
proudly. Never did I hear you
Complain of the pain
you brought from the hell
you left behind.
Forced memories.
Dark memories
locked in your heart
but you soon realized
life is too short to not
live it up! And
that you did –cabrón,
to the fullest!

Your wily smile
I'll always remember.
Yes, I know, I know
you meant well when you
playfully teased us all
you could never go wrong
with that high–pitched voice
and rowdy laugh.
Somehow you always
managed to bring us all
home –to our senses.

These memories I hold
vividly dear in my mind…

"Don't worry about me; I'm alright… coño, cabrón!"
were the last words
you left in my voicemail.
The tone and true meaning
of those final words will remain
just between you and me…

In the hoop of life all
good things must come full circle.
Peace, carnal… Peace is with you now…
And I'm happy for you.

**In memory of U.S. Army Sgt. David "Slim" Guerrero ,who was always proud to have served in spite of the adversities he faced coming home.*

BROTHER SHY (In Memoriam)

What's going on 'bro?
How are the streets treating you?
You all right?
Still spreading the Love?

These were the frequently asked
questions I would ask Brother Shy…

George McClinton, Shy… –Mr. Flowers (hee, hee)
always on the roll.
You had come this far
in spite of our age… always
spreading the Love! Yea,
you'd smile every time
I said that to you.

I'll never forget you Shy
for all the laughs and good times
but most of all
for saving my life –back in '69.
That morning in the wee hours
when you came out,
out of nowhere –like a Guardian
Angel to get me out of a bind
with some drunken strangers
determined to obliterate me…

As I told you on that recent day
(a few years ago) when
I saw you walking down
Ol' Eighteen Street
that I would NEVER
FORGET your stepping
up to the plate for me
when we met right
at that same corner
of 18th and Allport
facing St. Procopius (of all places).
It sure was a point of recognizance
For both of us…
after some 50 odd years!

I pointed with my index
finger to the spot
where I could still
see myself
as a teenager
on the ground
swinging my fists while
getting pounded
by those three drunk strangers.

You jumped in and lifted
My spirit. We joined forces
and brought Justice to the street.

Moments later, I remember
you asking if I was OK and
then saw you walking away
reassured all was well with me

You saved my life, my brother.
Letting me see another day…

Thank you Shy!
You were always blessed
always…by helping others
with an open heart and
no strings attached.

In spite of the adversities
you lived on… and I live on
forging our diverging paths
in our worldly lives and carried
on the best way we could…

I know you are up there
next to all your loved ones
and with brother Greg (who beat you
To the final punch –ha!)

Rest well Brother Shy.

FOUR O'CLOCK TORTILLAS

Two cups of flour,
two tablespoons of lard
(shortening will do as well
or butter if you so desire)

A teaspoon of salt,
half that of baking powder
and of baking soda.

Don't forget the tepid
cup of water; mix well.
Knead the contents
into an elastic dough and
cover it with a damp towel
and let it rest a while…

Come back later and
cut the *masa* into
fist-size baseballs.
Take the rolling pin and
flatten the dough balls
into thin roundish discs
Resembling yellow moons
and place them in
the family's pre-heated
ancient comal bought and
brought from Mexico
to Chicago.

All this I remember well…

Hot and fluffy pleasingly
aromatic tortillas.

The freshly-made
tortilla scent emanating
from ama's cocina
is now announcing
the arrival of
the odd-shaped
freckled round faced
tortillas on the kitchen table
stacked high like
a Toltec column
waiting to be consumed
in a disappearing act by
hungry little brown hands.

GRILLED ONIONS

One pork chop sand-
wich and
a Polish,
please.

Mustard
and plenty
of your
famous
grilled
onions
on both.

Here's a
sawbuck
and a fin
to cover
the cost
and you
can keep
the change.

I need
to be
gone be-
fore that
unforgiving
cop shows
up and
tickets my
car for being
double-parked
on Maxwell
Street where
a legal parking
space is so-o-o
very hard to find.

CHICAGO HOT DOG

Red hot, frankfurter
wiener, weenie
or just plain dog
steaming hot
set on a soft
and lightly
moist vapor-
heated poppy
seed bun.

Layered with
yellow mustard
diced onions
and fresh
tomato wedges.

One pickled
cucumber spear,
a couple of
sport peppers.
skip the neon
green piccadilly
relish (it's not for me).

That's one
Chicago dog
ready to go
all wrapped
in pearly white
wax paper
given to you
in a brown
paper bag…

But be mindful
and remember
never never-rr
ask for ketchup.

Leave it for
your freshly cut
deep-fried
french fries
that are often
included in your
timely order.

You can always
depend to
find your
Chicago-style
hot dog
twenty-four/seven
at your local
friendly and nearby
Chicago neighborhood
hot dog stand.

SUNDAYS IN THE PARK

When winter leaves and Spring
rolls into our neighborhood park
March winds and April squalls
rinse and scrub the park benches
and sweep clean the winding bike path.

Everyone knows a new season
of growth and rebirth is about to start again.
The tall maples and pruned crabapples
are eager to dress their naked arms
along with the daffodils and dandelions
in yellows and greens.

High up in an elm a cardinal announces in his
singsong that spring cleaning is overdue
while a cool breeze makes ripples
in the shallow grassy lagoon
and a flock of sparrows huddle
skipping and hopping in the puddles.

Above the fast-moving clouds
the sun takes a peek down below
at the backyard chefs dressed
in windbreakers and knee-length
cut-off baggy pants scanning the grass
to claim their favorite spot soon-to-be
shady in the neighborhood park.

Everyone knows the corn-on-the cob summer
is anxiously waiting its turn to arrive
once the May flowers bloom
And our baseball diamond and
the soccer field are ready to host
the annual opening Sunday
in our neighborhood park.

ZOOTOPIA

A pair of aging penguins
flap their arthritic wings
and slowly wobble down
the decaying neighborhood street.

They swear city water is
responsible for their aches
and pains but there's no one
willing to take the blame.

The local bank's reliable clock
blinks the hour of the day
And the liquor store's digitized sign
prompts the rushing herd

Of onlookers to note the customary
Immigration raid has gone sour
and postponed for a surprise
return the day after tomorrow.

There will be no crying hatchlings
tonight and a tired mother hen
and her newborn chicks
will finally get a night of solid rest.

Bus fare and cold sandwiches will
once again be ready before sunrise.
Tomorrow will be just another day
at the slaughter house.

Up the street
in a trash-covered empty lot
five adolescent crows have
skipped school and try to hide
and avoid being discovered.

They jiggle to and 'fro
and tease at each other's pride
As they compare their second-hand
black leather coats.

Across the way several silverbacks
veteranos with blistered hands lean
against the stalwart neighborhood
church's silent crumbling walls.

A troop of jobless baboons waits
for another day of dreams to end
leaving them hungry and with
empty pockets once again.

For now, down at City Hall
the newly elected walrus
In a pink tuxedo rests
his stumpy legs upon his shiny desk.

Sipping coffee while he stares
at the stars and stripes
pinned in his office wall
while his patronage sloths remain on task

Meanwhile, down State Street…

faded reelection banner sway freely
in the contaminated downtown air.

SNAKE IN MY FRONT DOOR

Who are you to come
knocking at my door
and spew your version
of the Lord
on the scanty grass
in my front lawn,
on my rain-soaked front
porch potted plants,
on my weather-stained
plastic bird feeders,
and sparrows hovering
over the tree in front?

Where did you get
the power to condemn
the paintings hanging
in my living room walls,
the kitchen aromas
permeating the air,
the echoes of my children
now gone to school and
my old car resting
in the street mulling over
many trips to the hospital
marked in its treadless tires?

Please keep your holy
quotes and paraphernalia
in the compartments of
your worn-out carpetbag.
Slither back into your
snaky surroundings.
It will be greatly appreciated
if you kindly not bother
to stop and knock on
my door next time you
come near my house.
Adios and have a blessed day.

DREAM BEYOND

Minimum wage.
Never-ending debt.
Meager meals.

WIC*ked* welfare.
Government cheese.
Pulverized eggs.

Fast food obsessions.
Clogged arteries.
Heart congestion.

Ramshackle housing.
Ubiquitous roaches.
Crafty mice (and rats).

Omnipresent drug scenes.
Insidious addictions.
Chronic disease and infections.

Piecemeal education.
Worthless political rote.
Mass domestication.

Jive-talking preachers.
Oppressive religions.
Quid pro quo

Politicos and demagogues.
Classism, racism, gender-ism
Isms and more isms… Status quo.

Say no. Enough is enough!

Dream Beyond!

SI SE PUEDE

Leave the neighborhood
They say.
There is no other way
They say.
You are doomed if you stay
They say.

But it really doesn't have to be that way…

Who says you can't
make it if you stay?
Elevate yourself above
fear-spreading hearsay.

Dream and achieve.
If you believe, you
will succeed and remain
safely in the place
your family and mine struggled
and forged many milestones
dreaming, toiling, and reaching
goals for you and for me.

Yes, you can survive
the relentless onslaught
of newcomers with their SUVs
their pedigreed dogs and
corporate eateries changing
the face of tell-tale streets
and claiming the neighborhood
that we learned to love and
hold dearly in our hearts.

Subdue your fears…

Find that needle
in your haystack
of possibilities
And get involved
in the shuffle and re-making
of your block and mine…

There's nothing wrong with that!

Remember a goal achieved
always starts as a dream.
Who says you can't achieve?
Yes it can be done!

So think locally and be part
of the unavoidable change
coming your way and
realize your own dreams.

The neighborhood may change,
but let it be with you in the quest
and be part of new and better days,

So, no matter what they say…

Keep in mind it can be done.

Yes, it can be done!

!Si se puede!

WE, TOO, ARE SINGING AMERICA

As we scrub your dishes, pots and pans
with skin-piercing detergents in the greasy
kitchens of your restaurants, hotels and grand chalets,
we too are singing, America.

As we clean your lawns, parks and highways
in brazen heat and bone-chilling winds
and make you proud of your streets and railroads,
we too are singing, America.

As we harvest your bounty under the scorching sun
in the bosom of your fertile fields while
breathing pesticides that permeate your fruited land,
we too are singing, America.

As we tile your floors and tar your roofs
and paint your walls with lead-filled hues
while my limbs grow numb and arthritic,
we too are singing, America!

As we fine-tune and lubricate your gas-guzzling SUVs
hand-wash and caress your sedans with the finest wax
my aching back and joints guarantee your gleaming cars,
we too are singing, America.

As we count and assemble your disposable widgets and gadgets
under artificial light and sweltering heat and floating ashes
inhaling the rancid indoor air of your sweatshops and factories
we too are singing, America.

As we splinter the veins of your mines in search of precious metals
in the cavernous bowels of your majestic mountain ranges
taxing my skin and lungs inhaling nauseating dust and gases,
we too are singing, America.

As we care for your prolific poultry and inbred cattle
in the viscera of your prodigious farms and ranches
surrounded by dusty silos, sloshing waste and squalor,
we too are singing, America.

As we march into your battlefields and global confrontations
and leave the indelible stain of my blood in your trenches
to uphold the inalienable rights given by your Constitution,
we too are singing, America.

As we toil proudly in the polychromatic hues and tones
interlacing the legacy of our ancestry, we bestow on thee
the transcendency of our Raza Cósmica's genome
anticipating the day, you become a rightful part of us…

I, too, am singing, **América!**

GLOSSARY

Atole—Beverage made with corn starch with added cane sugar, natural fruit flavors, chocolate, cinnamon, and vanilla

Agua fresca—Flavored and water made with freshly squeezed fruits, seeds and sweetened with cane sugar

Cabrón—Old goat, stud, bad dude

Café con leche—Café au lait

Camaradas—Comrades, best buddies

Cantón —House, shanty, the crib

Carnales—Brothers by blood or close-knit friendship

Charola—Handcrafted tray adorned with colorful flower and used to hold fruits or sweet breads on the dinner table

Coño—Term commonly used to express surprise such as: "Fucker!", "Oh, shit!", or "Damn!"

Día de los Muertos—Day of the Dead. An annual celebration held in November to remember and honor dead relatives.

Jarros—Cay cups or glass jars for drinking coffee or atole.

La Virgen Morena—Virgin of Guadalupe ("The Brown Virgin")

Lord of Mictlán—In Aztec/Mexica mythology, Lord or God of the Dead

Mezcal Mixteco—Liquor fermented and distilled from the agave plant; similar to tequila but with the obligatory added agave worm.

Mole—A sweet & spicy rich sauce made of chocolate, chiles, seeds, various culinary herbs and spices that is added to meats (primarily turkey, chicken, and pork).

Norteño—Of or belonging to the northern part of Mexico and the borderlands surrounding both Mexico and the United States.

Papel Picado—Punched paper banners made out of thin paper or plastic that are cut to give form to intricate designs and are used as party accents.

Pa' siempre—Forever

Polkeando—Dancing Tejano/Norteño polka-style

Raza Cósmica—The Cosmic Race. The visionary concept of racial evolution developed in 1919 by then Mexican Minister of Education Dr. José Vasconcelos in which he predicted the rise of a new and all-inclusive human race derived from the inter-mixing of all the existing races (African, Amerindian, Asian, and Caucasian) in Latin America with its principal evolutionary nucleus already evident and taking shape in Brazil and spreading from there to the rest of the entire American Continent.

Veteranos—Old-school dudes. The term is also used in referring to barrio elders and US military service veterans.

ABOUT THE AUTHOR

JOEL MÉNDEZ, originally from South Texas, migrated as a child to the Midwest with his parents, who were seeking work and a better life. Settling in Chicago's inner city, Joel grew up and came of age in the multi-ethnic and racially mixed, but by then mainly Mexican Pilsen Neighborhood community on the city's Near West Side.

Joel attended and graduated from the Chicago Public Schools and completed his undergraduate and graduate studies at the University of Illinois in Chicago (UIC) with degrees in Biological Sciences, Public Health, and Education. Working as a researcher, academic counselor, and administrator at the UIC Medical Center Campus, he also served as a science and mathematics educator and school administrator (K-12). He is a self-taught in creative writing and poetry and an amateur photographer. *Forty Poems for City Living* is Joel's first book.

CONTACT FOR BOOK PRESENTATIONS:
jjmendez007@gmail.com

LACASA Chicago Latino/a Publications

(order at www.lacasachicagobooks.org)

I. Books.

MZ [1]. *Mexican and Chicano Literature in Chicago: Transplanting Early Roots to the Barrios and Beyond. Chicago*. LACASA Chicago/ March Abrazo P.

MZ. *Defending Their Own in the Cold. The Cultural Turns of U.S. Puerto Ricans*. Champaign. U. of Illinois P. (Paperback edition 2020).

MZ. *U.S. Latino Literature: An Essay and Annotated Bibliography*. Chicago: MARCH/Abrazo. Out of print.

II. Editions.

Joel Méndez *Forty Poems for City Living: Pilsen-18th Street:* ***Pilsen-18th Street.*** Chicago. LACASA Chicago. MARCH Abrazo.

Pablo Ramírez. *Pocho Love. A Pilsen Heart Beats to Chicago Streets*. Chicago. LACASA Chicago. MARCH Abrazo.

Carlos Cortez. *Coyote's Song. Collected Poems and Selected Poems*. Ed. Carlos Cumpián and David Ranney. Chicago. March Abrazo P.

Sonia Báez Hernández, Anadeli Bencomo y MZ, coord. *Ir y venir: procesos transnacionales entre América Latina y el norte*. LACASA/Bravo y Allende.

---

[1] MZ=Marc Zimmerman.

Cardenio Bedoya, Flavia Belpoliti y MZ, eds. *Orbis/Urbis Latino: Los "Hispanos" en las ciudades de los estados unidos.* Houston. LACASA. 2008.

José Gamaliel González. *Bringing Aztlán to Mexican Chicago: My Life, My Work, My Art.* Introduced and edited by MZ. Urbana. U. of Illinois P.

MZ, ed. *José Gamaliel González. Documenting the Work of a Chicago Mexican Artist and Activist.* CD format, Chicago: LACASA. A book version in progress.

Aaron Kerlow. *El gran circo chico de nuestro mundito: Escritos y dibujos / The Great Little Circus of our Small World: Writings and Drawings.* Bilingual vol. intro. and ed. by MZ. Global Casa & LACASA Chicago, 2

John Pitman Weber and MZ, ed. *A Guerrero Named Guerrero: Taller than a Tall Mural.* LACASA Chicago.

MZ, ed. *The Mexican Experience in Chicago: Memories from the Early Years and Echoes in Our Time.* LACASA Chicago.

Antonio Delgado, (edited with MZ). *Taking Off in the City: Mexicans from Hull House and Pilsen Areas on Chicago's Near West Side, 1910-1960.* LACASA Chicago.

Illusions of Memory Autofiction books with Considerable Mexican Chicago Content:

MZ *Martín and Marvin.* LACASA Chicago.

MZ. *A Mexican Maze without Borders.* LACASA *Chicago.*

Made in the USA
Monee, IL
20 September 2023

43007267R00069